BY **Susan E. Goodman**   PICTURES BY **Lee Christiansen**

An Expedition

ON
THIS
SPOT

Back Through Time

Greenwillow Books

An Imprint of HarperCollins*Publishers*

THIS IS NEW YORK CITY.

New York hums and hurries, races and rumbles—from under its sidewalks to the sky up above.

Buried in the earth, the subway travels to all parts of the city. Each day it takes millions of people to work and school, to plays on Broadway, and to stores along Fifth Avenue.

Cars and buses drive down busy streets. Trucks and taxis honk their way up crowded avenues. In the sky above, airplanes are bringing even more people to the city.

About eight million people live here. There are so many New Yorkers that, if laid out head to toe, they would stretch all the way to California and back again. All these people help make New York one of the biggest, busiest cities in the world.

BUT ON THIS SPOT . . .

175 YEARS AGO . . .

New York was a different city. Horse-drawn carriages bumped their way over cobblestone streets. Oil lanterns lit up its nights.

Bakers and milkmen pushed their carts through the city. Some peddlers sold corn that was grown on farms along Fifth Avenue. Other peddlers sold water, because city wells did not have enough for everyone.

About 160,000 people lived in this New York, just enough, if stretched out in a line, to cross the neighboring state of Connecticut. There were chickens in almost every backyard. Mothers warned their children to stay away from the wild pigs that ran through the streets.

AND ON THIS SPOT . . .

A fort and its cannons guarded the city of New Amsterdam. Windmill blades turned round and round, providing power to cut logs into boards for new houses and sailing ships.

Fire wardens watched over the city's tall houses. Their leather buckets stood waiting to douse any blaze. After dark a rattle-watch took his turn on patrol. Walking city streets, he called out the hour, ready to sound his rattle at the first sight of danger. On the blackest of nights, when the moon was in hiding, every seventh house hung out a lantern to brighten his way.

Fewer than fifteen hundred people lived in New Amsterdam, but eighteen different languages echoed through its streets. Portuguese fur traders argued over prices. Dutch children shouted to playmates. French women visited with neighbors at the community well.

If all these people stopped talking and stretched out in a line, they'd form a human bridge between today's New York City and the Statue of Liberty in its harbor.

AND ON THIS SPOT . . .

4OO YEARS AGO . . .

A great forest grew, with walnut trees standing next to oaks and maples. Elk ate the grass. Bears gobbled blackberries from bushes and grapes from vines. Cougars and bobcats watched from the trees above.

The Lenapes hunted in this forest for deer and wild turkeys. In spring, they crossed through it to fish in their warm-weather campsites by the water. In fall, they followed their trails back inland to harvest corn and firewood. One of those trails, which stretched north and south, eventually became a street named Broadway.

AND ON THIS SPOT . . .

There was no forest at all.

Cold winds blew across rocky hills. The winds—and weather—were so fierce that plants could not grow very tall. Instead, some of them grew in dense mats that hugged the ground. Growing so close together helped these plants keep warm.

Each year, spring painted the hillsides in fresh, bright colors. New leaves splashed green against the brown branches of tiny birch and bilberry. Soft moss beds unfolded in velvet shades of jade and emerald. Flowers filled in the season's rainbow—dandelion yellow, saxifrage purple, and rhododendron red.

The arctic fox and snowshoe hare wore new colors as well. They shed their winter white for grayish-brown coats to blend with their springtime surroundings. The wooly mammoth, standing tall in the landscape, did not need to worry about camouflage.

AND ON THIS SPOT . . .

20,000 YEARS AGO . . .

The weather was much colder. Ice wrapped the landscape in brisk whites, frozen blues, and chilly greens.

In June, as in January, slow-moving rivers of ice called glaciers covered the entire countryside. These glaciers were so thick that they would have buried today's tallest buildings. They were so heavy, the earth's crust sank beneath their weight.

AND ON THIS SPOT . . .

190 MILLION YEARS AGO . . .

A forest baked in the heat of endless summer. Evergreens shared the tropical sun with royal ferns that arched up as tall as trees.

Pterosaurs spread their furry wings and swooped in the hot sunshine. Fabrosaurs nibbled on horsetail plants. An ammosaur stretched his long neck to get at some ginkgo leaves. Suddenly a dilophosaur crashed through the trees and bushes. Her sharp fangs glistening, this dinosaur was looking for a different kind of meal.

AND ON THIS SPOT . . .

220 MILLION YEARS AGO . . .

A group of *Coelophysis* fought over a dead fish near shore. Meanwhile a phytosaur slipped into a shallow lake. When he opened his jaws, nearly 170 teeth swam toward a giant amphibian called a metoposaur.

Volcanoes smoked on the horizon. Clouds of steam billowed upward, rushing to meet the clouds in the sky.

Lava spit out of some volcanoes; it oozed and burped from others. Sometimes the lava flowed in boiling rivers of melted rock, so hot it took years to cool. Now and then, glowing droplets shot up from the earth, hundreds of feet in the air, just like water in a giant fountain.

AND ON THIS SPOT . . .

300 MILLION YEARS AGO . . .

A mountain jabbed the clouds with its peak. This mountain was so high that plants and trees could not grow all the way up its sides. It was so high that the air up top was thin and hard to breathe.

This mountain was part of a range taller than any mountains in the United States today. Peak after peak wore crowns of snow against the blue sky.

AND ON THIS SPOT . . .

370 MILLION YEARS AGO . . .

Waves rolled across a tropical sea.

Coral reefs grew up from the sea floor below. Gardens of sea lilies swayed in the water like flowers bending in the breeze. But these sea lilies were really animals that strained tiny creatures out of the water for food.

Giant squid-like animals, housed in shells, used their arms to walk on the sea bottom. Their arms also grabbed trilobites and other animals for dinner.

Large sharks swam in these waters. They were hunted by an even bigger fish. This *Dinichthys*, or "terrible fish," was about thirty feet long. Its jaws could crush a victim with just one snap.

BUT ON THIS SPOT . . .

540 MILLION YEARS AGO . . .

There was no sea. There was no mountain. There were no animals or insects or green leaves reaching for the sun.

This spot was only rock, rock as far as the eye could see. Except for a dusting of algae, this spot looked a lot like the surface of our moon.

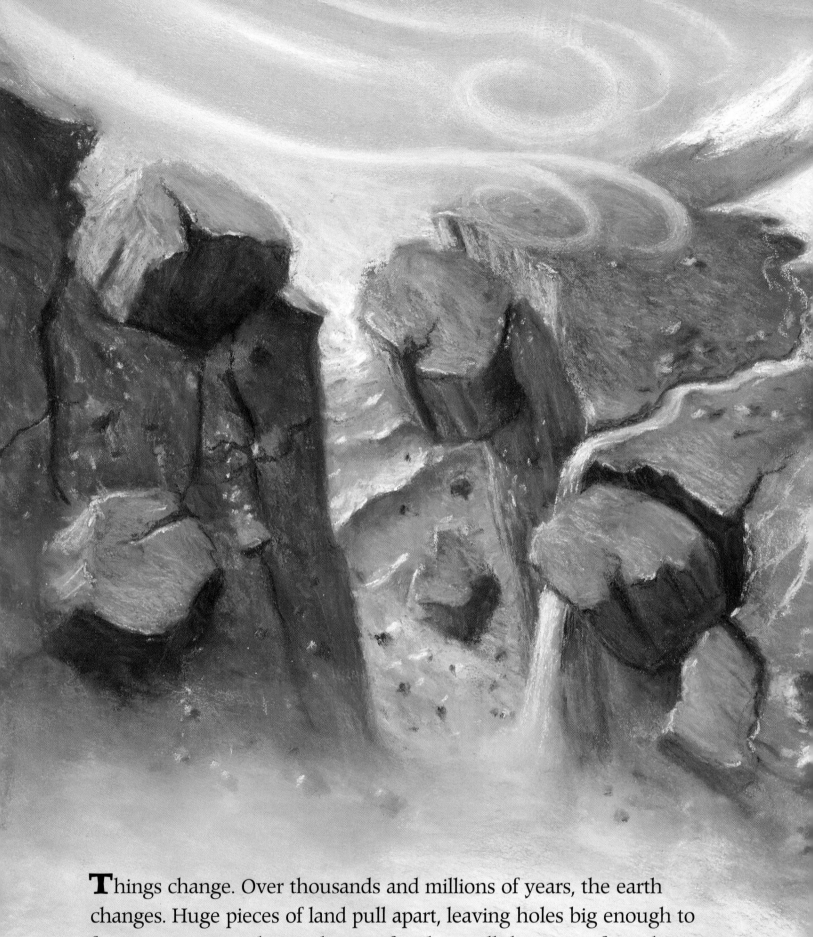

Things change. Over thousands and millions of years, the earth changes. Huge pieces of land pull apart, leaving holes big enough to form oceans. Seas dry up, leaving fossils to tell the story of another time.

Huge pieces of land press together, and mountains push toward the sky. Giant glaciers bulldoze some of those mountains. Wind and water crumble others, one rock at a time.

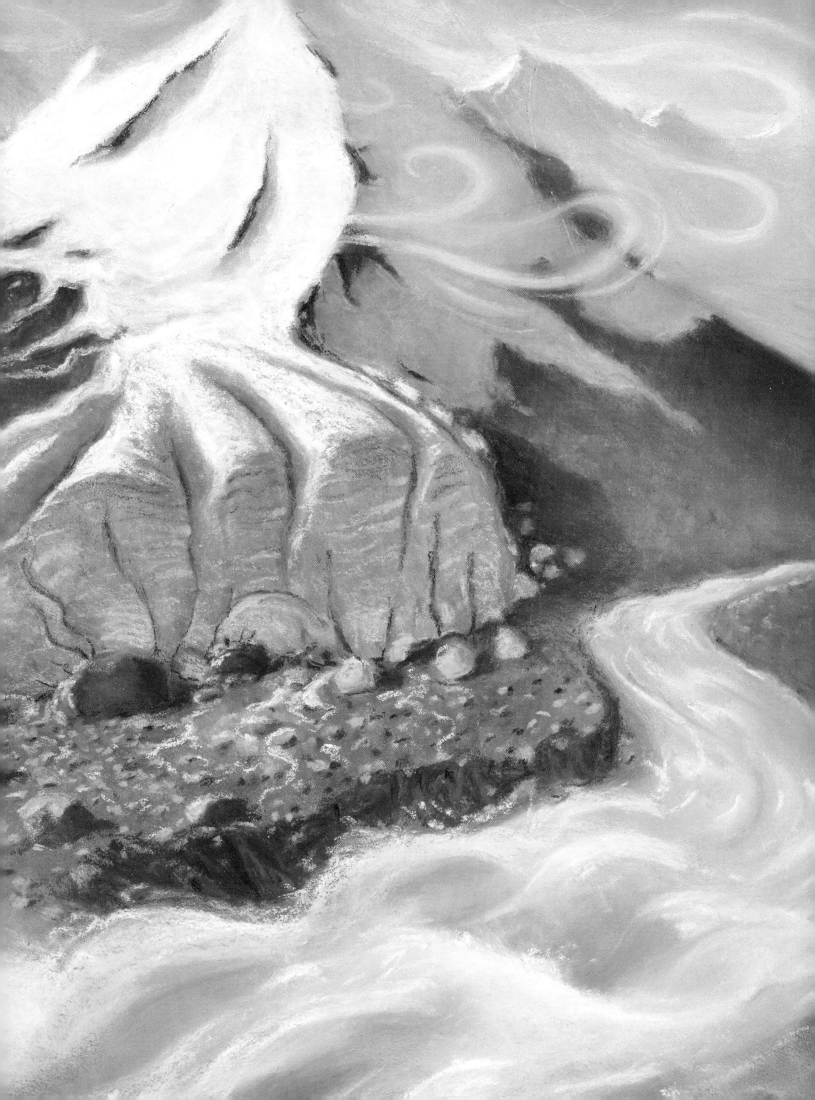

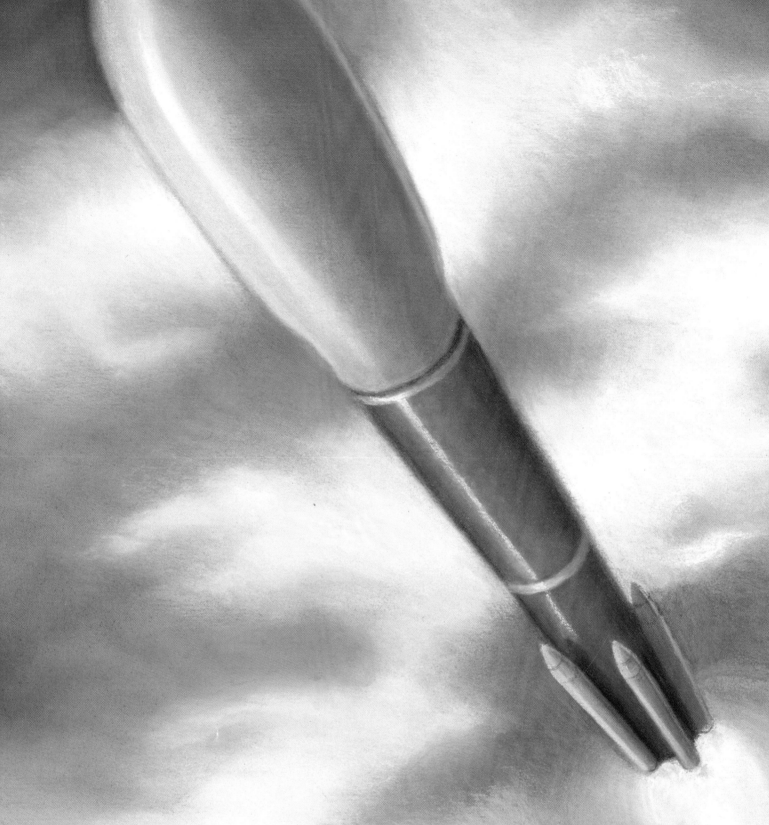

Over hundreds and thousands of years, people's lives change as well. Some of their cities disappear into history. Others, like New York, are still growing and changing.

Long ago, kites were the only things people could fly high into the sky. Today, we launch spaceships. Our world—and the way we live in it—will continue changing. First a little, then a little more. Life will be quite different when your children have children of their own.

Think of the moon that lights up our night. Astronauts have walked its surface, but going there still seems as distant as a dream.

In a hundred years, who knows?

ON THAT SPOT . . .

TIME LINE INFORMATION DATING
FROM TODAY TO 544 MILLION YEARS AGO

ACKNOWLEDGMENTS:

My thanks to the many experts who helped me understand "this spot" over time, among them Anne Tyrrell, Ron Birch, and Drs. Ed Landing and Norton Miller of the New York State Museum; Stephanie Betancourt of the National Museum of the American Indian, Smithsonian Institution; Eileen Morales, Manager of Collections Access, Museum of the City of New York; Margaret Carruthers at the American Museum of Natural History; Brett Bennington of Hofstra University; Paul E. Olsen of Columbia University; and Rich Krueger at Dinosaur State Park.

This book has evolved, just like New York City. Thanks to Deborah Hirschland, Elizabeth Law, Janet Coleman, Lisa Jahn-Clough, and Liza Ketchum for their editorial insights. Lee Christiansen, thanks for bringing New York of every era so beautifully into view. And a heartfelt thanks to the crew at Greenwillow—especially Chad Beckerman, Rebecca Davis, and Virginia Duncan—for caring so much about this book every step of the way.

—*Susan E. Goodman*

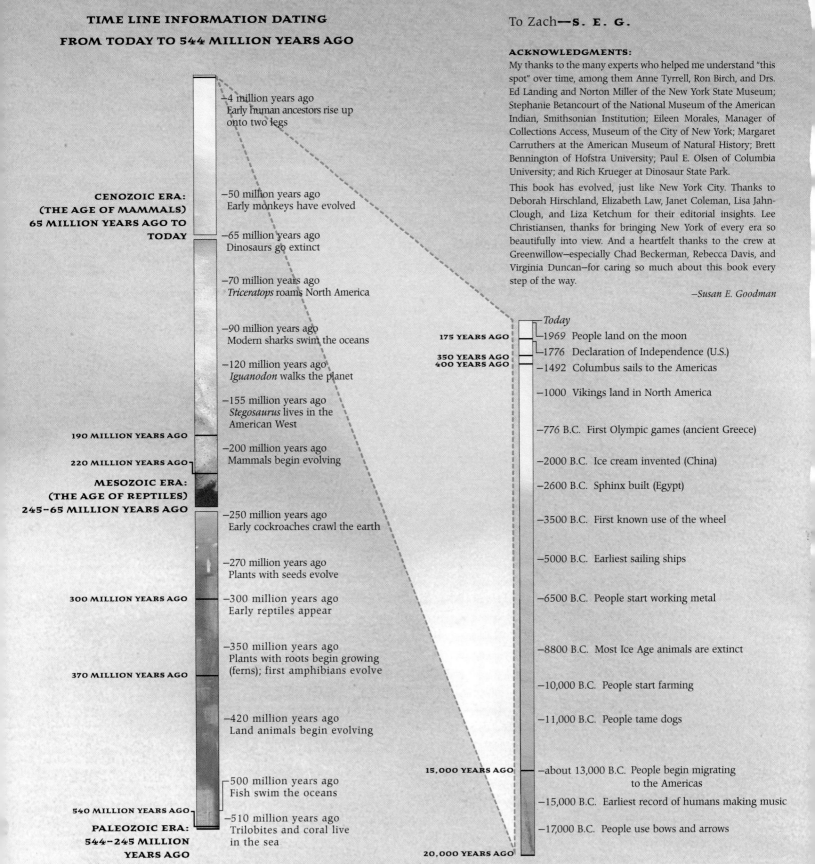

CENOZOIC ERA:
(THE AGE OF MAMMALS)
65 MILLION YEARS AGO TO
TODAY

–4 million years ago
Early human ancestors rise up
onto two legs

–50 million years ago
Early monkeys have evolved

–65 million years ago
Dinosaurs go extinct

–70 million years ago
Triceratops roams North America

–90 million years ago
Modern sharks swim the oceans

–120 million years ago
Iguanodon walks the planet

–155 million years ago
Stegosaurus lives in the
American West

190 MILLION YEARS AGO

–200 million years ago
Mammals begin evolving

220 MILLION YEARS AGO

MESOZOIC ERA:
(THE AGE OF REPTILES)
245–65 MILLION YEARS AGO

–250 million years ago
Early cockroaches crawl the earth

–270 million years ago
Plants with seeds evolve

300 MILLION YEARS AGO

–300 million years ago
Early reptiles appear

–350 million years ago
Plants with roots begin growing
(ferns); first amphibians evolve

370 MILLION YEARS AGO

–420 million years ago
Land animals begin evolving

–500 million years ago
Fish swim the oceans

540 MILLION YEARS AGO

PALEOZOIC ERA:
544–245 MILLION
YEARS AGO

–510 million years ago
Trilobites and coral live
in the sea

175 YEARS AGO
350 YEARS AGO
400 YEARS AGO

–Today
–1969 People land on the moon
–1776 Declaration of Independence (U.S.)
–1492 Columbus sails to the Americas

–1000 Vikings land in North America

–776 B.C. First Olympic games (ancient Greece)

–2000 B.C. Ice cream invented (China)

–2600 B.C. Sphinx built (Egypt)

–3500 B.C. First known use of the wheel

–5000 B.C. Earliest sailing ships

–6500 B.C. People start working metal

–8800 B.C. Most Ice Age animals are extinct

–10,000 B.C. People start farming

–11,000 B.C. People tame dogs

15,000 YEARS AGO

–about 13,000 B.C. People begin migrating
to the Americas

–15,000 B.C. Earliest record of humans making music

–17,000 B.C. People use bows and arrows

20,000 YEARS AGO

On This Spot: An Expedition Back Through Time
Text copyright © 2004 by Susan E. Goodman.
Illustrations copyright © 2004 by Lee Christiansen.
All rights reserved. Manufactured in China by South China Printing Company Ltd.
www.harperchildrens.com. Pastels were used to create the full-color art. The text type is Poppl-Pontifex.
Library of Congress Cataloging-in-Publication Data
Goodman, Susan E., (date). On this spot / by Susan E. Goodman ; pictures by Lee Christiansen.
  p. cm. "Greenwillow Books." Summary: One spot in New York City is traced from present day back to millions of years ago.
ISBN 0-688-16913-9 (trade). ISBN 0-688-16914-7 (lib. bdg.)
1. New York (N.Y.)—History—Juvenile literature. 2. Natural history—New York (State)—New York—Juvenile literature. [1. New York (N.Y.)—History. 2. Natural history—New York (State)—New York.] I. Christiansen, Lee, ill. II. Title.
F128.33.G66 2004 974.7'1—dc21 2003010148
First Edition 10 9 8 7 6 5 4 3 2 1

Greenwillow Books